Elevate Your Network

25 Keys to Building Extraordinary Relationships in Life and Business

Jake Kelfer

Elevate Your Network
25 Keys to Building Extraordinary Relationships in Life and Business

Jake Kelfer
Cover Design by Jonah Kelfer

Warning – Disclaimer

The purpose of this book is to educate and entertain. The author or publisher does not guarantee that anyone following the techniques, suggestions, tips, ideas or strategies will become successful. The author and publisher shall have neither liability or responsibility to anyone with respect to any loss or damage caused, or alleged to be caused, directly or indirectly by the information contained in this book.

Dedication

To my network: Thank you for being part of my journey! I wouldn't be where I am today without the support you've given me or the relationships we've developed.

To my family: Thank you for all that you do for me. I love you all more than you know!

Motivate and Elevate Others!
"Give the gift of giving"

Elevate Your Network
25 Keys to Building Extraordinary Relationships in Life
and Business

Networking is the ultimate key to success. In a world run by people, relationships drive happiness, success, wealth and more. In this book, networking is defined as the creation of genuine, mutually beneficial relationships in all aspects of life. When you build and develop these types of relationships you will have more positive opportunities in your life.

Sign up for Jake's email list at:
www.jakekelfer.com

To purchase bulk copies of *Elevate Your Network* at a discount for your school, team, or organization, please contact Jake and his team at
books@jakekelfer.com

JAKE KELFER

Jake is a high-energy inspirational speaker who creates lasting impact! He uses stories, humor and audience interaction to inspire, engage and elevate the audience. He is always willing to work with his clients and tailor his presentation to best serve their audience.

One of America's Rising Young Speakers!

Here's what people have to say:

"Jake Kelfer has one on the most engaging and fun motivational messages I have seen for students and faculty alike!"
– Rachelle Modena, Deputy Sector Navigator for Small Business

"Jake Kelfer is an amazing, dynamic speaker who exploded onto the scene with an extreme amount of energy and enthusiasm. He captivated an audience of over 1,500 Virtual Enterprise students where they hung on to every word of his inspirational message of hope and hard work."
– Jake Stuebbe, Virtual Enterprise Northern California Regional Director

"Jake has you ready to run through a wall when he's done talking with you."
– Scott Horwitz, Indiana University

"He is super! His work with the Lakers, his personal journey, and his abundant energy make his presentation relevant, vibrant, and memorable. You won't be disappointed."
– Robyn Hissam, High School Teacher

To have Jake speak at your school or next event, please email *jake@jakekelfer.com* or visit
www.jakekelfer.com/speaking!

Table of Contents

Author's Note

Hello there!

I'm Jake Kelfer and thanks for picking up your copy of *Elevate Your Network*. I hope you are ready to build and develop extraordinary relationships!

I am a bestselling author, high-energy inspirational speaker and founder of the Professional Basketball Combine. I am on a mission to inspire and ELEVATE millions of people on their own journey to achieving their definition of success.

One of my passions, and yes you can have multiple, is speaking to students and staff and inspiring audiences full of people. As a young speaker ready to change the world, I love sharing a message that will influence and ELEVATE people in their life, career and beyond!

To be honest, I love building relationships. I love meeting new people and learning about their journey. The world is filled with amazing people who, when given the chance, can positively impact and influence your life, and you theirs.

I credit a lot of my current success to networking and building mutually, beneficial relationships. In everything that I do, I aim to provide value while doing so with a smile on my face.

In 2015, I graduated from the University of Southern California with a degree in Business Administration, a minor in Sports Media Studies, and an emphasis in Entrepreneurship. Many of the relationships I built in college have been the foundation for my support system as well as the base for my growth.

After graduating, I worked with the Los Angeles Lakers in the Corporate Partnerships division where I was able to work with the team during Kobe Bryant's last season. I secured this job after connecting with multiple employees who went to USC.

In 2016, I created My 12 Month Journey which was the idea that for every month in 2016 I was going to do an activity or try something that scared me or that I claimed I never had time to do with the hope of inspiring people to take action and maximize their time. The twelve activities were:

- Krav Maga - Israeli Self Defense
- Hip Hop Dancing with Brittany Glodean
- Book Marketing for *Elevate Beyond*
- Cooking
- Meditation and Stretching
- Fitness Challenge – Insanity
- Euro Trip to Amsterdam, Rome, Florence, Barcelona and Berlin
- Learn Basic Chinese
- Healthy Eating
- Daily Vlogging

- Create a Sales Funnel for an Online Course
- Push Up Challenge

In May of 2016, I launched my first book, *Elevate Beyond: A Real World Guide to Standing Out in Any Job Market, Discovering Your Passion and Becoming Your Own Person.* *Elevate Beyond* is an Amazon bestseller in three categories and is currently being used in high schools and universities across the country.

At the start of 2017, I created the Professional Basketball Combine which is a secondary NBA draft combine for draft prospects. Each prospect has the chance to compete in front of NBA personnel and achieve their dreams of playing professional basketball.

In October of 2017, I started my Elevate America tour with the intention of building my businesses, connecting with people in person, and living in different locations across the US for weeks at a time. This trip gave me the chance to live in and visit 11 cities and states over the course of 8 months including places such as Michigan, New York, Florida, Nashville, Vegas, and Texas.

In May of 2018, I concluded my Elevate America tour with year two of the Professional Basketball Combine which grew to new heights and featured some incredible players. The event was highlighted in media across the globe and I had the chance to connect with people from all over the world.

And now, *Elevate Your Network* is here for you.

All of these experiences have taught me so much about life and business, but no matter what I am doing or where I am traveling to, people always win.

I wouldn't have had the chance to do all of these experiences without my ever expanding and developing network. I am constantly meeting new people, hearing more stories, creating introductions, starting collaborations, and doing everything I can to elevate my network.

This book is all about networking and I want to be in your network. I want to be a part of your journey and help you anyway that I can. I encourage you to connect with me and share your successes as you apply what you learn from this book.

Website: www.jakekelfer.com
Email: jake@jakekelfer.com
Facebook: Jake Kelfer Journey
Instagram: @jakekelfer
Twitter: @jakekelfer
Snapchat: @jkelf
LinkedIn: Jake Kelfer
YouTube: Jake Kelfer

I hope that as you read this book you will learn about the power of networking and how to create and develop relationships that will change your life. By the end of this book, I hope you will feel more confident and ready than ever before to ELEVATE your network and continue on your journey to achieving your definition of success both in life and career.

Let's ELEVATE!

Kelf Key #1: Be Authentic. Be Genuine. Be Sincere.

"I had no idea that being your authentic self could make me as rich as I've become. If I had, I'd have done it a lot earlier."
– Oprah Winfrey

"Be genuine. Be remarkable. Be worth connecting with."
– Seth Godin

"If you want the cooperation of humans around you, you must make them feel important – and you do that by being genuine and humble."
– Nelson Mandela

Authenticity is everything when it comes to building relationships. People respond well to other people who are authentic and sincere. There's a reason Barack Obama inspired millions of people during his tenure. There's a reason John Wooden is one of the most respected and successful coaches in history. There's a reason Oprah is a hero and role model to millions. Each speaks their truth and is authentic in their own way.

Authenticity means speaking from the heart. It means telling the truth and maintaining your integrity. In order to build relationships that lead to new business, jobs, friendships, or lifelong partnerships, you need to be sincere when you communicate.

Some of you may be thinking, *how can I be authentic and sincere while I am simultaneously trying to network with someone with the goal of acquiring a new job or client?* That's a valid question; but if you are authentic, genuine, and sincere, and those qualities come through in your communication, it doesn't matter what your objective is, because who you are as a person will speak volumes. By being sincere, you give yourself a chance to be seen for who you are—and not for what you want.

Look, we all want something in life, whether it's a new job, a promotion, a new client, a spouse, or more friends. That doesn't mean we need to exploit or take advantage of others to get there. Instead, we can choose to be authentic, genuine, and sincere. By choosing to focus on fostering these positive attributes in yourself, people will respond better to you and will be more inclined to give you what you ultimately wanted in the first place.

One of my favorite entrepreneurs is Scooter Braun. Scooter is the founder of SB Projects, which is an entertainment and media company with ventures integrating music, film, television, technology, and philanthropy. He represents some of the world's largest superstars, including Justin Bieber, Ariana Grande, Kanye West, Usher, and plenty more. His accolades and achievements are great—actually, unbelievable—but what makes Scooter one of my favorite people is how he connects with others. He is 100% true to himself, whether it's in an interview or a new venture, with his family, or even posting on social media. When I look at Scooter, I see someone who focuses on being authentic, genuine, and sincere, and as a result he has appeared in *Time* magazine's "100 Most Influential People" and is one of the most respected businessmen of his generation. People from all over the world want to work with Scooter, and it all started with him building his brand and business through authenticity, believing in his duty to help others, and creating mutually beneficial partnerships.

When it comes to building relationships, think about the long term, not the short term. If you think in the short term, you are more likely going to place your immediate interests above the value of building relationships. If you think in the long term, you are more likely going to cultivate incredible relationships and appreciate the process at the same time. Networking is about building relationships and making sure that both parties benefit from each other.

Just because someone isn't ready to work with you or hire you today doesn't mean they don't know someone who can or will want to in the future.

When you connect with someone, are you being 100% authentic, or are you trying to impress them? Are you being genuine and speaking from the heart? Are you being sincere?

Elevate Your Network in Action: Find any person in the world with whom you want to speak. It can be an executive at your company, a colleague, or someone you bump into on the street. Walk up to them and just say hi and smile. Introduce yourself and ask them how their day is going.

Kelf Key #2: Meet People!

"A simple hello could lead to a million things."
– Unknown

"The secret to getting ahead is getting started."
– Mark Twain

"You can't get to the top of the mountain without taking the first step."
– Unknown

It might seem really obvious that I am including this as a Kelf Key, considering my book is all about connecting with others, but this is a pretty important foundation to networking and relationship building. Get off your butt and start meeting people. All it takes is one person to believe in you to make a difference.

You will never get your dream job or sign a career-changing client by sitting around idly. You are reading this book because you want to become a better networker and communicator. So, if you want to improve your relationships, stop making excuses that you are too busy. The only way you can build deeper relationships is to meet people, so go out there and start doing it.

I know meeting new people can be nerve-wracking. I get it, and for some of you, this is the hardest part. You don't have to meet 100 people all at once, but you do need to start. I promise you that if you begin meeting people, you will not only actually make connections, but it will become easier and easier for you. You will get better at talking to new people and over time, you might even grow into enjoying the process of converting a random stranger into a lifelong friend or business partner.

The worst that can happen when you meet someone new is that they don't want to talk to you. Big whoop. There are seven billion other people in this world, and a whole lot of them would love to talk with you. The more people you meet and talk to with authenticity and sincerity, the more success and relationships you will have.

If you aren't sure where to start or how to expand your reach, here are five ways to meet more people:

- Attend professional conferences
- Eat lunch with a new colleague in the office
- Join a networking group or mastermind
- Start a study or project collaboration group
- Get involved with a local organization or philanthropic endeavor

Whether you are an executive meeting with a college student who is looking for a job or an entrepreneur meeting a potential client for the first time, keep the following in mind: whenever you meet someone new, they may very well be just as nervous or excited as you.

Part of meeting people is putting yourself out there and setting yourself up for success. I am always thinking about networking and meeting new people. A while back, I was practicing a speech for an upcoming speaking gig at a Starbucks in Los Angeles. I know that Starbucks is a destination for people to work independently or have quick meetings, so I came prepared. On the chance I'd meet a basketball fan or sports business professional, I wore a polo from the NBA Summer League. I purposefully wanted to seem accessible and to give someone the opportunity to reach out and strike up a conversation with me who maybe wouldn't have done so otherwise.

Within an hour of being there, the person sitting next to me asked me if I worked in basketball. I told him I worked in the business but that I was really just wearing this shirt because it was super comfortable and I loved the NBA (I didn't tell him that I wore it for exactly this reason). He started asking questions and we hit it off talking about sports and our professions. We realized we had a lot in common, and by the end of that random encounter, we were making plans to have dinner with some of his connections.

As of today, the person I met at that random Starbucks in Los Angeles is now a close friend and mentor.

So whenever you meet or approach people, be yourself. Don't be afraid to ask a question or give them a compliment. When you meet someone for the first time, give a firm handshake, look them in the eyes, and smile.

This will exude confidence, but even more than that, it will help both you and the person you are meeting relax and feel more comfortable with each other.

Be willing to meet people and turn strangers into friends. On the flip side, give someone a reason to approach you. When you are open to meeting people, good things will start to happen.

Elevate Your Network in Action: Sign up for and attend a networking event. Go to a career fair. Go to a mixer in your local community. Sign up for a professional conference. Ask a friend for an introduction to a colleague or to set you up for a date. Arrange a meeting with someone in your company whom you've never met. Go to a coffee shop—and once you arrive, take a deep breath, count to three, and go for it.

Kelf Key #3: Add Value

"Strive not to be a success, but rather to be of value."
– Albert Einstein

"Saying hello does not have an ROI. It's about building
relationships."
– Gary Vaynerchuk

"No one ever got poor by giving."
– Anne Frank

Always, always, always add value to someone else's life. The more value you add, the more irreplaceable you become. When striving to build relationships in your life and business, you should focus on helping others achieve success. When you can make someone else better or happier because of your efforts, you will not only build relationships, but these relationships will be incredibly strong and meaningful and will lead you to amazing opportunities and experiences.

If you are trying to get a job, a promotion, or a new client, or just trying to keep your employees happy, adding value is one of the best ways to increase the depth of your relationships. Employers and recruiters want to see candidates that are passionate and willing to do whatever it takes to positively impact the company. Bosses and executives want to see that employees are making the lives of their customers and their colleagues better. Clients want to see that you are making their experiences and lives easier.

Start small. Say "please" and "thank you" and do tasks no one else wants to do. Show up early and leave late. Send an email to a contact and ask if there is anything they need assistance with. Walk up to the new person in the office and introduce yourself with a welcoming smile. If you know someone has to leave early for personal reasons, offer to finish their work for the day. Look around at the people in your inner circle and ask yourself, *what can I do to elevate the group?*

These suggestions are applicable to everyone, from the intern who's on her first day to the executive who's a leading expert in her field.

Sergio Millas, the digital marketing director of HallPass Media, makes it a priority to add value in everything he does, in and out of the workplace. Even though he's one of the head people in a company that serves clients like adidas and NBA Summer League, he still does the little things. When interns come to work an event, he welcomes them and shows them exactly what needs to be done so they can feel confident with their assignments. When one of his team members needs to handle personal business, Sergio encourages them and steps in for them. He understands what it means to help others out. When there is a huge task and no one seems to know how to handle it, Sergio takes the time to create a solution and then shares that solution with everyone so the team can get the credit.

One of my favorite ways Sergio adds value, though, is through his relationships outside of work. He always focuses on what he can do for his wife and his daughter, while at the same time always finding ways to help an aspiring sports business professional learn about the business. Sergio constantly focuses on how to add value to the lives of people around him, which has helped him become a widely respected and trusted person in the sports industry. I know all of this because he is one of my greatest mentors and someone whom I look up to very much.

A professor at the University of Southern California once told me that in order to make a name for yourself, you have to add value—so much value that you become an irreplaceable asset. This advice has stuck with me to this day, and now I am sharing it with all of you.

Gary Vaynerchuk, who is quoted at the beginning of this chapter, says to follow the rule of 51/49. He means to give more than you take when building relationships.

In every aspect of your life you can add value. You can add value in your family life by telling your family you love them. You can add value in your friendships by doing something nice for someone you care about. You can add value to your financial situation by promising to save money each month and whenever you can. You can add value to your body by working out and eating healthy. You can add value in your professional life by being proactive about a task and taking initiative.

Jon Chepkevich is a senior associate at PricewaterhouseCoopers (PwC) who has an extreme passion for the game of basketball. One day after work, he connected with me and asked if he could do some scouting for the Professional Basketball Combine. He didn't ask for anything in return other than a chance to be involved and show me what he could do. I appreciated the gesture, did my research, and decided to give him a shot. Not only did he end up sending me some incredible scouting reports, but he became one of the main team members in assisting with talent evaluation for the Professional Basketball Combine. What started out as a simple ask to provide value turned into an incredible friendship, partnership, and career opportunity.

There's no shortage of ways you can add value and be genuine in your approach. Unfortunately, too many people see adding value as a transactional approach.

It's fairly common to send an executive, decision maker, CEO, coach, or potential mentor a cold email that's great until the end, when you might conclude with, "Let me know if there is anything I can do for you." While the effort of you wanting to add value to someone is there in that sentence, you should think about the position you're putting them in. Picture yourself in their shoes and ask yourself, *are they really going to go out of their way to answer a cold email and then think of something I can do to help them?* Probably not. This gesture is appreciated, but it's going to be more of a nuisance than not for someone to figure out how you can help.

Instead, you should do your research and rather than *ask* how you can add value, you should *show* them how you can add value. Actions speak louder than words.

I'm guilty of this mistake. I've done it before and while my intentions are great, it doesn't get the job done. The better way to accomplish your goal is to figure out a specific way you can add value and present it to the person you are trying to get in contact with.

Let's say you are trying to build a relationship with a potential business partner. Instead of focusing on asking them what you can do and hoping for a response, take initiative and make an introduction to another person who would be a good connection to your potential partner. Another way you can add value immediately is by quoting someone in an article and then sending it to them thanking them for the inspiration. By doing this you are showing them that you are here to add value and that you want to create (or grow) the relationship.

Other times, a potentially valuable contact will receive an email that says, "If there is anyway you can help me out, I'm more than happy to help you out in any way that I can." Again, the contact might appreciate the effort here, but it is not enough. Even though this emailer might have the greatest intentions for reaching out, he or she is essentially writing, "If you help me, I can maybe help you." Authentic relationships aren't transactional!

I want to make it very clear, though, that it is okay to finish an email or conversation with, "Let me know if there is anything else you need" or "Let me know if there is anything else I can do." When you are already in conversation with someone, this is an appropriate way to continue developing the relationship and offering your time and services.

When you are reaching out for the first time to someone, your focus should be on showing value and trying to create the relationship rather than trying to ask what you can do for someone.

Think about your interactions with people, customers, and companies. Are you adding value? Is the person or company better off because they met you? How do you impact the company's bottom line? What do you do to make sure customers have a better experience when they work with you?

Elevate Your Network in Action: Write down the following questions and hang them up in your room or office for a daily reminder.

- **What can I do to help others?**
- **How can I add value to someone's life today?**

The next time you interact with someone, don't just ask if you can help them; take initiative and show them how you can help them.

Kelf Key #4: Be a Good Listener

"Most people do not listen with the intent to understand; they listen with the intent to reply."
– Stephen R. Covey

"When you talk you are repeating what you already know. But if you listen, you may learn something new."
– Dalai Lama

"The mark of a good conversationalist is not that you can talk a lot. The mark is that you can get others to talk a lot. Thus, good schmoozers are good listeners, not good talkers."
– Guy Kawasaki

People love to talk about themselves. Let them! Listen to what someone has to say and encourage them to talk about themselves. When you do this, you gain valuable insight and learn a lot about them. Better yet, the other person will appreciate your willingness to listen and be more willing to continue developing the relationship.

The strength of a relationship is based on the level of comfort, trust, and enjoyment you get from the other person involved. When you ask questions and listen, you build that comfort and trust.

Let me put it to you this way. The more questions you ask, the more you can learn about another individual. The more you listen to their answers, the better you will be

21

able to formulate your responses, because you will have listened to and processed all they said rather than just heard the words. The better your responses, the more engaging and sincere you are. The more sincere you are, the more they trust you. The more they trust you, the deeper the bond becomes. The deeper the bond becomes, the more likely they are to have your back, feed you opportunities, and support your life endeavors.

When you listen to someone and focus on processing the information, you will find that you remember more details. You can use this information for future follow-up and communication. You can use this information to figure out a way to add value to their life, so that you don't have to ask them how.

Also, when you listen to someone and focus on asking thoughtful questions and responding with depth, you may learn something that you didn't know previously. You may be able to connect them with someone else, or even be able to relate to them on a completely new level.

Ideally, all you thought you were doing originally was asking questions because you were genuinely interested in listening to what another person had to say. What you ended up doing was laying the foundation for a fantastic relationship. Don't underestimate the power of asking questions and being a good listener.

As Greek philosopher Epictetus says, "We have two ears and one mouth so we can listen twice as much as we speak." The greatest connectors in the world focus on listening because they want to show others they care and are living in the present moment with them.

Have you ever had someone that makes you feel like a million bucks? You know, those people who, whenever you talk to them, leave you feeling great at the end of the conversation. Well, be that person that makes someone else feel confident and valued.

There are a few people in my life who are incredible listeners and because of that, they are people that I always want to be around. They ask me questions about myself, my work, my dating life, everything. What separates them from the rest is that they ask questions with the intention of really listening to what I say and responding based on my answer. This often leads to them asking further questions that dive deeper into the topic. By doing this, these people make me feel great and often, it leads to more clarity or ideas on my part.

When most people meet a new person or see someone they know, they ask the person how they are doing. Before that person even answers the question, the speaker has usually already moved on to the next person or question. Asking good questions and being an active listener is about being there for someone else and genuinely caring about their response.

Maya Angelou said it best: "People will forget what you said, people will forget what you did, but people will never forget how you made them feel." Being an active listener leaves the people you converse with feeling valued, wanted, loved, heard, and appreciated.

Elevate Your Network in Action: Practice listening. Ask your parents, your children, your friends, or your colleagues several questions and focus on what they say. Ask follow-up questions that are triggered by their responses to your first few questions. Watch how much they appreciate this and how much you actually learn.

Kelf Key #5: People are People. Love is Love. Compassion is Compassion.

"My mission is to not merely survive, but to thrive; and to do so with some passion, some compassion, some humor and some style."
– Maya Angelou

"If you would be loved, love and be lovable."
– Benjamin Franklin

"No act of kindness, no matter how small, is ever wasted."
– Aesop

I think it's safe to say that we are all different. We come from different backgrounds; we speak different languages; we have different beliefs; we have different senses of humor; we like different foods; we want to have different jobs; we have different ideas of love.

But...

At the end of the day, I think we can agree that we all share some similarities. We all want to be loved; we all want to feel valued; we all feel good after being complimented; we are all trying to figure out the journey of life. We are all PEOPLE.

I know that approaching a stranger, prospective employer, boss, high-level executive, or celebrity can sometimes be intimidating. It is important to remember that we are all people with the same basic desires. We all like to be complimented, smiled at, and loved.

Think about a time when someone praised you. How did that make you feel? If you are like most people, it made you feel great; it might have even made your day. Give people compliments, no matter their title or status. Don't suck up to someone because you want something, but do give authentic and sincere compliments.

The more you show love, compassion, and respect to others, the more people will appreciate you and want to be around you. Whom would a company rather hire: the person who is filled with respect and honest compliments, or the person who only cares about their own success? Whom is a potential customer going to choose: the person who makes them feel comfortable and valued, or the person who is purely trying to get their money? Whom would a company rather work with: a teacher who cares for her students and wants them to succeed, or a teacher who has an ego and is difficult to deal with?

I'll never forget this one time, when I was working with the Los Angeles Lakers, I was in the elevator heading down to the court for the game, and Jerry West was in there with me. The attendant didn't know who Jerry was and therefore wasn't going to let him down to the court level.

Side note—how can you work at Staples Center and not know who Jerry West is?! I mean, he's the frickin' NBA logo...

Anyways, instead of being nervous or intimidated around Jerry because of who he was, I told the attendant that he was my guest and I was escorting him down to the court. The attendant approved and Jerry was allowed access to the court. When we got off the elevator he thanked me and we chatted for a couple minutes before he went to his courtside seats.

The point of this story is simple. Regardless of someone's status or position, treat everyone with respect and they will return the favor. This is an experience I will remember and share for the rest of my life. It never would have happened if I was too intimidated to stand up for Jerry West and suggest that he was my guest.

Just as people come in different shapes and sizes, religions and ethnicities, and genders and colors, love and compassion manifest in different ways. In addition, we all respond to love and compassion in our own ways. Any act of love, kindness, or compliment can have a direct and immediate positive impact on someone else. In Viktor Frankl's *Man's Search for Meaning,* he reflects on a time where he was given a small piece of bread from one of the guards and it moved him to tears. If someone gave you a little piece of bread when you were hungry, you'd probably thank them but not think too much about it. In this situation, Frankl was in a concentration camp, and for a guard to give him a piece of bread was not only a miracle, but it was a life-altering event for him at that moment in time. Frankl explains that it wasn't just the bread that moved him to tears: "It was the human 'something' which this man also gave to [me]—the word and look which accompanied the gift" (*Man's Search for Meaning*, 108).

You never know what type of day someone is having or what someone is going through, so it's always best when building relationships to be a kind-hearted person and show love and compassion.

Every interaction you have in your life comes with a choice: a choice to show love, kindness, and compassion. You can't always control how someone else feels or how they talk to you, but you can always choose how you treat others.

Elevate Your Network in Action: At the next professional event you attend, walk up to the host and thank them. Walk up to a stranger and introduce yourself. If you don't know what to say, it can be as simple as saying, "I appreciate you taking the time to put on this event. The turnout is spectacular."

If you want to be a little more forward and honest, find something from the conversation or draw from their appearance and compliment them. You can say, "That's a nice shirt," or, "It's great to meet someone so passionate about their job. I'm excited to get to know you and the company better." See how these comments play out and what happens next.

Elevation Recap

Kelf Key #1: Be Authentic. Be Genuine. Be Sincere.
Kelf Key #2: Meet People!
Kelf Key #3: Add Value
Kelf Key #4: Be a Good Listener
Kelf Key #5: People are People. Love is Love. Compassion is Compassion.

What is one thing you can do to be authentic and intentional with your network?

_____

_____

_____

_____

Where are 3 places or events you can meet someone new?

_____

_____

_____

_____

What is something you can do right now to add value to a friend? A colleague? A boss? An employee?

_____

_____

_____

_____

Who was your last conversation with and what did you takeaway from it?

_____

_____

_____

_____

What was the last compliment you gave someone? What is something you can say to someone who looks like they are having a tough day?

_____

_____

_____

_____

Kelf Key #6: Have a Plan

"Failing to prepare is preparing to fail."
– John Wooden

"If you don't know where you are going, you'll end up somewhere else.
– Yogi Berra

"I've always considered myself to be just average talent and what I have is a ridiculous insane obsessiveness for practice and preparation."
– Will Smith

You need to have a plan when you network. You need to know what your objectives are, who you want to build relationships with, and what companies you want to connect with. You need to know your talents, strengths, weaknesses, and what you bring to the table. Prepare yourself so that when you arrive at a networking event or conference or you meet someone new, you can build a great relationship.

This isn't the minor leagues. You're in the majors now—so if you want to reach the highest level of networking success, you need to create a strategy to help you get there.

Your networking plan should be a set of actions you can take that will get you closer to achieving your definition of networking success. If you want to connect with someone at Google, you need to create a networking plan that is targeted to achieve your objective.

Actions in your networking plan to create a relationship with someone at Google might look something like this:

- Connect with five Google employees through LinkedIn, email, referrals, etc. this week who work in the department(s) you want to learn more about
- Follow Google and their employees on all social media platforms
- Set up one informational interview with someone at Google
- Prepare a list of questions to ask a Google employee
- Practice your elevator pitch in case someone asks you about yourself—more on this in Kelf Key #13
- Understand current trends in the tech space, especially within the segment of Google you are looking to work with

By no means is this a full networking plan, but it is a great place to start.

If you are in the early stages of your networking journey, start small by planning what questions you might ask someone upon first meeting them. If you are a networking veteran, plan how you can maximize your experience with every person you meet or really get to know the people you set out to meet. Clearly set your intentions for each encounter and figure out ways you can provide value to every interaction between the two of you.

All of us have a unique style of communicating, so there is no one way to create your plan. Design your strategy based on your personality and your objectives.

If you know you have a lot of energy and love meeting people face-to-face, try to incorporate more in-person interactions in your networking plan.

If you prefer to stay in a single location and communicate over the phone or online, figure out ways to be creative in your communication.

If you are going to be on the road and know there are people or companies you want to connect with, set up meetings in advance and combine online networking with face-to-face meetings.

In today's world, you will also want to figure out your social media plan. Are you going to use LinkedIn? Twitter? Facebook? Snapchat? Instagram? YouTube? What are you going to do on each of these platforms to network? For me, I love using LinkedIn for professional networking, so I allocate a certain amount of time each week to making new connections and setting up meetings. No matter how many people I have relationships with at any given time, having an up-to-date plan is a huge part of my growth and development and should be for you as well.

I make it a point to figure out the best way to connect with someone. I know that people are extremely busy and don't always have the time to meet for lunch or jump on a call. With that in mind, I try to figure out what platforms or methods of communication are most effective for the individual I am trying to connect with. If I know someone is very active on email, I will go that route. If I see someone is going to be traveling to a conference, I might try to attend the conference and meet up with them in person.

When I was a sophomore in college, I wanted to be a sports agent. I was in the education phase of learning and meeting as many agents as possible, trying to understand the business and the type of people who are successful in the agent world. One night during an entrepreneurship class, Pete Carroll, head coach for the Seattle Seahawks and former USC football coach, was scheduled to speak at USC. Not only was I extremely excited to hear Pete speak, but I figured that his agent might also be in attendance to help facilitate the details and logistics of the night. Agents are often responsible for helping coordinate speaking engagements and off-the-field or -court opportunities.

With this in mind, I did some research and figured out who Pete Carroll's agent was pretty quickly. While I was listening to Pete share some amazing stories and relive his top USC moments (which was an incredible experience), I kept an eye out for his agent. At the end of the night, I finally saw him as he was leaving the building. I knew this was my chance to get in front of him, so I sprinted out of the building and ran up to him. I introduced myself, telling him that I was an aspiring agent and that I would love to learn more from him and set up a time to get to talk about what he did and how he had secured Pete as a client. I didn't ask for anything that night except his card to follow up. He was more than thrilled that a young college student had run up to him to meet him. Remember, people love to feel complimented, and my coming to him made him feel recognized. He gave me his card and told me to follow up with him the next day. I did, and within a few weeks, we were able to have lunch and get to know each other.

Having a plan and being clear on what you want to achieve through networking will help you capitalize on situations and create more opportunities for yourself. I was super nervous to approach Pete's agent, but I didn't know the next time I would be this close to him. I knew that if I wanted to connect with more agents, I had to try and take advantage of every opportunity. Do I expect everyone to run after someone and introduce themselves? No. But, I do expect you to create a plan to help you maximize your networking success based on your communication style and preferences.

I know that in order to continue building the Professional Basketball Combine and to make it the best event it can possibly become, I have to cultivate relationships in the basketball world with everyone—including agents, college personnel, NBA personnel, media members, overseas teams, sponsors, potential employees, trainers, and many more groups of people. The Professional Basketball

Combine is a secondary draft combine that gives players an opportunity to compete in front of decision makers and turn their dream of playing professional basketball into their reality.

In order to build all these relationships, I have to put myself in a position to meet lots of people and include it as part of my plan. That's why I decided to attend the NCAA Final Four and Portsmouth Invitational Tournament in Portsmouth, VA. I know events like these attract the exact people I have to meet with and further develop my relationships with. Since I know this, I can incorporate traveling to these events as part of my networking plan leading up to the Professional Basketball Combine.

It doesn't stop after just meeting or reconnecting with people. It continues with providing value and maintaining these relationships so that by the time of the Professional Basketball Combine and in the following years, these relationships will be stronger and may even lead to new introductions and relationships.

I am willing to make the investment and travel all across the country to have the chance to build relationships face-to-face. I want people to know that I am willing to do whatever it takes to meet with them because I value their time and thoughts. Before I do this, I figure out how both my event and I can provide value to each stakeholder I am meeting with. I tailor my message so that when I come across new people or connect with colleagues I can 100%

authentically show them how the Professional Basketball Combine will add value to their life and business.

Not everyone who reads this book will be willing to invest in multiple cross-country trips within a few weeks' span, and I understand that. I think we all have different networking objectives, but I also believe that having a plan is imperative to helping you reach your own definition of networking success.

Think about how you can help people in the present or in the future. Think about how you can cultivate relationships that are mutually beneficial. Think about everyone you want to know and why you want to know them. Incorporate these networking objectives into your plan.

Once you have a plan, begin to execute it.

Are there any upcoming networking events at your school, company, or local community? How many people do you want to connect with this month? Is there a deadline for your next sale, for when you need a job, or for when you want to get your promotion?

Elevate Your Network in Action: Commit to networking. Take out a pen and paper and answer these six questions:
1. **How many people do you want to connect with per week?**
2. **Whom do you want to connect with?**

3. Why do you want to connect with them?
4. What is your objective and how will reaching out to these people help you get there?
5. How do you plan on connecting with these people and what platforms will you use?
6. What are you willing to do in order to meet these people?

Now, execute that plan.

Kelf Key #7: You Never Know Who You Are Talking to Until You Know

"Don't judge a book by its cover."
– Unknown

"Be curious, not judgmental."
– Walt Whitman

Treat people the way you want to be treated. Cliché? Of course. True nonetheless? Absolutely.

Talk to everyone and be polite to everyone. Don't judge people based off the way they look or the person you think they are. Get to know them personally and make your own opinions about them. When you do that, great things can happen—like meeting someone who can change your life, or someone whose cousin works at your dream company in your dream job, or even the person who can introduce you to your biggest client.

When I was in college at the University of Southern California, I made it a priority to get to know as many people as I could. I didn't just talk with business students because I was a business major. I talked to future doctors, engineers, entrepreneurs, finance students, athletes, communications students, actors, and everyone in between.

Just because someone comes from a different background, studies a different subject, or works in a different industry than you do doesn't mean you can't or shouldn't get to know them.

I can't tell you how many times these conversations led to me learning so much about others' stories and backgrounds. Some had parents who were the CEOs of huge corporations or had their family name on a building. Some were great people on scholarship doing whatever it took to enjoy their time at USC so they could provide for their families once they graduated. Had I been more selective in whom I talked to, I would have missed out on meeting some incredible people and making some incredible connections.

Grant Baldwin, a well-known youth speaker and founder of The Speaking Lab, understands this concept better than anyone else. When he was first starting out as a speaker, he spoke to what he thought was a normal audience. He didn't know who was in the audience other than the general demographic. At the end of his talk, a woman came up and introduced herself as the wife of the national director for the organization. They got to chatting and it turned into a huge growth opportunity for Grant and his business. Grant didn't know initially who was in the crowd or who the stranger was, but he gave the best talk he could and things worked out for him.

Everyone has a story to tell and, until you truly get to know someone, you might never fully understand their story or where they come from. Approach each person with the mindset that they might be the most amazing individual you have ever met. When you meet someone for the first time, keep an open mind. Whether you are at a networking event, in a Facebook group, or even working within an organization, meet as many people as you can and try to get to know something about them that is deeper than surface level. You'd be surprised at how interesting people are and how many new connections and relationships you will make just by talking to more people and keeping an open mind.

In the movie *The Internship* with Vince Vaughn and Owen Wilson, both actors play the role of interns at Google. As two grown men, they struggle in the beginning to be accepted and to fit in with the other, more youthful interns. Their team doesn't even want to sit with them at lunch, so Vince and Owen's characters end up sitting next to a guy wearing headphones and seemingly ignoring everybody. They say hi, get no response, and continue to eat their lunch. Later in the movie, Vince's character is studying to learn how to answer questions for an upcoming intern challenge. While he is studying, the guy with headphones comes up to chat with him. Vince soon realizes that the guy is not that great at communicating with people, and the guy in turn realizes that Vince is not very good at understanding how to answer questions about Google. "Headphones," as he is called in the movie, helps Vince learn the technical side of things, while Vince helps Headphones have a good conversation with a friend. At the end of the movie, we find out that this quiet, socially awkward guy with headphones is actually the head of search for Google and assists Vince and Owen in winning full-time positions.

Yes, I just made a reference to a fictional movie. And yes, I loved this movie. But, the important takeaway is that you never know who you are talking to until you know. You never know who someone is or who they might know or how they might be able to help you until you know. Don't judge someone by the way they look or by who you expect them to be. Find it within yourself to see people as people and give yourself a chance to experience another's beautiful life journey!

Elevate Your Network in Action: Say hi. Smile. Hold the door for someone. Eat lunch with a stranger. Ask questions. Invite the new kid or employee to hang out. Sit next to a different person every class.

Kelf Key #8: Make Yourself Available

"The greatest gift you can give someone is your time. Because when you give your time you are giving a portion of your life that you will never get back."
– Anonymous

"Relationships take time and effort and the best way to spell love is T-I-M-E."
– Rick Warren

"It's not about having time. It's about making time."
– Unknown

When it comes to building authentic, genuine relationships, it is vital that you are available and accessible. I understand that some of us prefer to keep to ourselves while others of us want the whole world to be able to reach us. However you feel is totally okay.

With that said, if you want to build authentic relationships and elevate your network you must set aside time to connect with others. You can do this as simply as setting aside 15 minutes a few times throughout the week to dedicate to meeting new people or fostering your relationships.

Make your social media profiles public, especially your LinkedIn. The more visible your social media is, the more chances you have of people reaching out to you. The last thing you want to do is keep your contact information private and miss out on a potential lead trying to contact you. On the other hand, if you do decide to make your social media public, be aware that everyone will see anything you post.

Relationships aren't built overnight, so give yourself time to create them. When you are looking to connect with someone, give them several options for when you can talk or meet for an informational interview. You want people to know that you are willing to work with them and can adapt to help make their lives easier. Give yourself every advantage you can by making yourself available.

Then, as you develop the relationship, continue to be flexible and willing to make time for them. I am not advising you to be available at all times or to change your schedule to make time for someone else every time they ask, just to consider being flexible and a team player, especially when it comes to investing in a relationship with someone you value.

I don't care who you are—you can't build a network by being unavailable all the time. You need give yourself time and energy to connect with others because, at the end of the day, this will be a huge component to maximizing your relationships and their development.

Time is our most valuable resource and how we use it will dictate our quality of life. When you're busy and your schedule is full, you have to be more selective with how you spend your time.

I know that some of you reading this have jam-packed schedules, so it is extremely important for you to network with intention. This is when having a networking plan and a personal definition of networking success comes in handy.

Elevate Your Network in Action: Set aside 15 minutes a day for networking. Make it part of your daily routine. Give multiple options of availability when scheduling informational interviews and calls with prospective contacts.

Kelf Key #9: Be Patient and Understanding

"Patience is bitter, but its fruit is sweet."
– Aristotle

Relationships take weeks, months, or even years to develop. Whether you are the person reaching out or the person being reached out to, try to be understanding of other's situations. Not every email will get a reply, and not every conference will generate new business. If we only focus on the short-term and immediate impact, we will miss out on long term opportunities and meaningful relationships.

I can't tell you how many times I've sent an email or left a voicemail only to never get a reply. I've had this happen with CEOs of large companies and I've had it happen with entry-level student employees at universities. It sucks. But it doesn't necessarily mean that the person I reached out to isn't interested in connecting with me. It just means they might be busy, the email got lost in their inbox, or I have to find another way in.

In situations like these, it is important to be patient. Give the person some time to respond to you before reaching out again or giving up. If you haven't heard from them in a week, I recommend following up with another email or method of communication.

Since the time I wrote *Elevate Beyond,* I've had hundreds of people tell me how being patient during the job process gave them an advantage over the other candidates. They didn't take it personally when a company told them they needed more time or when someone they wanted to connect with didn't reply. They didn't annoy the recruiter or immediately freak out when they didn't hear back. Instead, they were understanding and focused on being prepared for when the phone finally rang. They took the time to continue reaching out, finding new people to connect with, and preparing for interviews.

There is a huge difference between being persistent and being annoying. Sending a follow-up email qualifies as being persistent as long as you continue to be authentic and sincere. If you immediately ask for something or are focused on what you can gain rather than creating a mutually beneficial relationship, that is annoying; in fact, not only is it annoying, but your chances of receiving a reply go way down.

I've seen people send an email and then send a follow-up within 24 hours. That's annoying. I've seen people send an email and confirm its receipt a week later. That's persistence.

The following story is a major no-no in networking. Never send someone a cold email and in that first email ask if they can introduce you to their network or give you a job. Who the heck do you think you are? This is one of the fastest ways to have someone never respond to your email. Personally, when someone does this to me, I explain to them that this is not the most productive way to approach the situation and I encourage them to reconsider their outreach and focus on mutual gain. I don't want my colleagues, or anybody else this person is reaching out to, to receive the same type of inauthentic communication.

If you are trying to reach someone who is established in their field or perhaps a guest speaker from a panel you attended because you think there is room for a partnership, keep in mind that they likely receive a lot of inquiries for networking opportunities or product pitches. Don't get upset and give up right away if they don't respond. Understand that they might take some time to reply. Set a reminder for yourself to reach out again and follow up. The best thing you can do is to be patient and understanding, but also persistent—which is why you should set yourself a reminder for when to reach back out. The worst thing you can do is to send an email the next day asking for more. Life is crazy! People can't always reply right away when it's most convenient for others. They have their own lives. It might take time, but they will get back to you when they can; and if they don't, that's what the follow-up is for.

If you are reaching out to your employees, it's just as important to be patient and understanding. Even though they may be expected to reply to certain outreach or requests quicker, as a leader and cultivator of relationships, you have to be patient and understanding and work with them.

Chris Henderson, a graduate of Syracuse University, was applying to do his senior capstone project with the New York Knicks. Though the capstone project wasn't beginning until the start of the year, Chris made initial contact with the Knicks marketing team months in advance. He was being proactive and showing his interest, but due to company policy, Chris had to wait to hear a final decision about whether or not he got the capstone until October. Instead of heavily pursuing other options, Chris trusted the relationships he made at the company, continued to follow up, and understood that the process takes time. While Chris was obviously anxious to hear the outcome, he focused on what he could control and respected the company's policy and process. His patience eventually paid off and he landed his dream senior capstone months after the initial contact was made.

In today's digital world with technology at our fingertips, we've come to expect people to reply immediately. We assume that because we are always on our phone or email that everyone else should be as well. We also tend to feel that our request is the best request on the table or the one that should immediately warrant a reply.

People are busy; it's part of life. You are going to send emails, offer deals, leave voicemails, or request LinkedIn connections and not hear back for weeks at a time. It's important for you to not take this rejection personally. As a matter of fact, most people appreciate the follow up, because then they know you are serious and ready to network. They will see your commitment and dedication and you will already appear more impressive in their eyes.

Elevate Your Network in Action: Be patient. If you do not hear from someone right away, give them a week and try again. Practice with your professors, family members, friends, and colleagues.

Kelf Key #10: Ask Your Friends and Family for Referrals

"When someone else's happiness is your happiness, that is love."
– Lana Del Rey

Don't be shy. Your friends and family are almost always willing to help. You just have to ask.

Sometimes we try to keep our personal lives separate from our professional lives, and I totally understand that. At the same time, it is 100% acceptable to ask your friends and family, people that you love and trust, for referrals or introductions that might help you advance your career and improve your relationships.

Think about it like this. Do you ask your friends for introductions to the cute girls or guys you see at a bar? Absolutely. The same should go for business and professional relationships. Remember, if you are authentic and sincere, the relationship will develop organically. Sometimes we just need a push—and that's what our friends and family are for.

When I first started growing my speaking business, writing books, creating a website, and everything else I do, the first thing I did was ask my family and friends in these specific communities for referrals to anyone in the industry who might be good for me to talk to. I went directly to the people I love and trust the most to ask for their help. They were more than happy to help me and, because of that I have been able to find new mentors and create new partnerships.

This same mentality can apply when starting a new company or trying to build better relationships with your colleagues, employees, or bosses. If you know of someone you want to speak with or a company you want to work with, ask your friends and family if they know anyone who could connect you. Maybe they will, maybe they won't. But, if you never ask, there's a 100% chance you'll never know.

We are not on this journey alone. We all have people that we can turn to when we need help. Even if you don't have a great family dynamic, you can ask your friends, counselors, professors, or colleagues for help. It's okay to be vulnerable and need help along your journey to success. I like to say that you can achieve more when you work with and help others than you can on your own.

Elevate Your Network in Action: Think of five people you want to connect with. Pick your best friend, mentor, or a family member you trust and ask if they know any of those people or anyone that works at the company where they work.

Elevation Recap

Kelf Key #6: Make a Plan
Kelf Key #7: You Never Know Who You Are Talking to Until You Know
Kelf Key #8: Make Yourself Available
Kelf Key #9: Be Patient and Understanding
Kelf Key #10: Ask Your Friends and Family for Referrals

What is your number one networking goal to achieve in the next month?

_____

_____

_____

_____

Have you ever had someone be totally different than you expected them to be? Who? What was different?

_____

_____

_____

_____

Where can you find time in your schedule to reserve for networking? Morning? Afternoon? Evening?

_____

_____

_____

_____

Who are the last 5 people you reached out to but haven't heard back from or connected with in a while?

_____

_____

_____

_____

Who in your family and friend group would you ask for help from first? List all people you would feel comfortable asking.

_____

_____

_____

_____

Kelf Key #11: Do Your Research

"Research is creating new knowledge."
– Neil Armstrong

When you are getting ready for an upcoming event, planning for an informational interview, preparing for a job interview, or rehearsing for a sales meeting, always do your research.

You should always focus on researching the person or people you are meeting with, the company they work for, the industry they work in, previous hires or deals they've made, and trends in their space.

When you research the person you are meeting with, make sure to check out their social media profiles. Is there anything that you can immediately connect with? Do you have anything or anyone in common that you can bring up? What schools did they attend? Do you know people from the same hometown? Is there an area of interest you can talk about in your meeting? Does the person you are meeting have a certain clothing style that you can relate to or comment on? Can you tell anything about their personality that may help you shape the conversation?

Outside of looking at someone's social media, see what they do. Try to find out what they are good at, what they struggle with, and what they are trying to achieve.

If you can learn more about someone before meeting with them or seeing them again, you can ask better questions and show more genuine interest.

Once you research the person, make sure to also look up the company they work for or the scope of work they are involved in. Are they an entrepreneur? Is the company thriving or is it on a hiring freeze? What was the person's last major career move or deal they landed?

Before you go into a meeting or enter an event, make sure you research trends across the relevant industries. It is very impressive when you can walk into a meeting and be knowledgeable about an industry that the other person cares so much about. It makes you appear more prepared and shows that you did your research—which will not go unnoticed.

Doing research can only help you be more prepared. A colleague of mine was once on his way to meet with a company for a potential new collaboration. Unfortunately, he didn't do much research on who was going to be in the meeting. Upon arriving at the building, someone accidentally cut him off as they were trying to turn into the office parking lot. He was already cutting it close on timing, so this pushed him over the edge. He freaked out and started yelling at the person in the car in front of him. When he walked into the meeting, the first person he saw was the guy he had yelled at. Let's just say the rest of the meeting didn't go so well.

Had my colleague spent the time to do his research or just remembered to always be respectful, he might have been able to avoid this situation.

Here are a few ways you can utilize your research.

If you have an informational interview set up with someone, you can use your research on the interviewee to prepare questions at a deeper level, which shows that you actually care about getting to know the person. This will likely result in you receiving better answers and therefore gaining more information that could help you with your networking objectives.

If you have a job interview coming up, you can use your research to show you are serious about the interview and committed to getting the role. You might even be able to bring up something from your research and experiences in your interview to help make the meeting more conversational. When you do that, you change the agenda from a Q&A to a conversation, which increases memorability and success rates.

If you are thinking about expanding your network or adding another connection on LinkedIn, you can use your research to customize your connection request, making it more personal and more likely to start a genuine relationship.

If you are trying to impress your students and you work in a high school or college setting, learn about pop culture references that your students know. If you can relate to them, they will feel more comfortable with you and will be more likely to work with you and to pay attention.

Remember, in all of these situations, research allows you to ask questions and build a relationship based on interest, sincerity, and trust.

When you do your research before reaching out, you are able to relate to someone right off the bat. Sometimes when I do my research my planned dialogue may change depending on what I find to be the person's interests, alma mater, or whatever other detail about them which I think might make the conversation go better.

For example, if I know someone is a Trojan, I can start the conversation off with a football score from the previous week. At the very least, I can say "fight on," and that might lead to us talking about our college experiences. You never know what might connect or resonate with someone, but if you do your research, you are setting yourself up to elevate your network.

The more you know more about someone, the easier it is to find a way to connect with them and pique their interest. I'm not advising you to stalk someone, but I do believe that you should try to learn more about someone as a way of showing genuine interest. Find some form of common ground and use that to build your relationship. As you get to know them, you will develop more shared experiences and similar interests and the relationship will blossom.

You've heard the saying "knowledge is power." Well, I say that's not entirely true. Knowledge is the vessel to power. Taking that knowledge and applying it is the key to unlocking power. As you conduct your research, focus on what you are learning and how you can utilize it. Just doing the research isn't going to make your relationships stronger. How you apply that knowledge is where you will differentiate yourself from others.

Elevate Your Network in Action: Google the person you want to reach out to or are meeting with. Check out their LinkedIn profile. Jot down a few notes about that person that you can bring up to increase the depth of the conversation and the power of your outreach request.

Kelf Key #12: Face-to-Face Connecting is Best

"Electric communication will never be a substitute for the face of someone who with their soul encourages another person to be brave and true."
– Charles Dickens

"The most important thing in communication is hearing what isn't said."
– Peter Drucker

Face-to-face connecting is the #1 way to build authentic, meaningful relationships. Why? Because you get to see the whole package. You get to see the other person's body language, feel the emotions, hear the tone of their voice, gauge their objectives intuitively, and listen to what is spoken.

Connecting face-to-face is the best opportunity to get to know someone in a quick yet intimate fashion. I always prefer to set up my meetings in person. I love having 15+ minutes of undivided attention with each person focused only on one another and how we each can add value to the other.

If you can get a meeting with your target person or client, do it. This is one way to make a memorable first impression and be remembered throughout the hiring or sales process. Better yet, you will be able to see how they act, look, and talk, and use your findings for future meetings.

When you meet face-to-face with someone, you might be able to pick up on their social tendencies and get a feel for what they like to hear. If you notice their face light up when they talk about sports, then you can infer that sports are important and of interest to them. Now, the next time you speak with them, whether it is to follow up or develop the relationship or in an interview, you can bring up sports because you know they are passionate about that particular topic. You never would have been able to pick this up unless you met them in person and saw their reaction in live time.

A huge reason for why I packed my bags and went on my "Elevate America" tour across the country for both my speaking business and the Professional Basketball Combine was to meet people in person. My relationships were great online and over the phone, but I knew there was no substitute for meeting someone in person.

By traveling across the country not only did I get to see a different side of America, but I had the privilege of fostering new relationships and taking my online relationships to the next level. This has led to more business and opportunity for me.

When I went to Syracuse, for example, I was able to meet people I had only worked with online. One of the main people I was able to bring an online relationship to life with was Nicole Imbrogno, the internship coordinator for Falk College's Department of Sports Management. We had built a great relationship through our communication over Skype and email, but in the few hours I spent on campus, we were able to elevate our relationship to the next level. We joked around, fed off each other's personalities, and got to know the person behind the keyboard. Since we met in person, our communication has been stronger and we have been able to provide even more value to each other by sharing content and supporting each other on our journeys. We have a different appreciation for one another because we actually know each other now. We know our in-person personalities, not just our online personalities.

Think about all the relationships in your life. Which ones are the most meaningful? How did they become that way? More likely than not, your best relationships come after talking in person. They come after spending time with an individual. While other forms of communication such as emailing, texting, or social media are great to start or even develop a relationship, spending time face-to-face advances the relationship and makes it real. There is influence and power in face-to-face communication that is unmatched in other means of communication.

Did you know 93% of all communication is non-verbal? 55% is body language, 38% is the tone of your voice, and 7% is the spoken word. Your ability to connect with others in person will drastically help you build more connections, both from an intellectual and emotional standpoint.

Elevate Your Network in Action: Practice communicating in person with a friend, family member, or colleague. If you don't have any friends or anyone you feel comfortable doing this exercise with, refer to Kelf Key #2 and meet people. Or, practice in front of a mirror. Ask your friend, family member, or colleague to give you feedback on the vibes you give off in conversation. Ask someone with whom you attend a networking event to give you feedback along the way. Be willing to adapt and grow.

Kelf Key #13: Elevate Your Elevator Pitch

"The purpose of an elevator pitch is to describe a situation or solution so compelling that the person you're with wants to hear more even after the elevator ride is over."
– Seth Godin

"If you can't explain it simply, you don't know it well enough."
– Albert Einstein

Every interaction is an interview. Every time you speak to someone new or speak to someone again, you are being interviewed. It is your job to always present yourself in an authentic way—a way that represents how you want people to view you. A lot of times, the best opportunities come when you least expect it. That's why you need to have your elevator pitch prepared. You have to be able to talk about who you are and what you are trying to accomplish in about 30 seconds.

Imagine you are at a Starbucks and someone asks you what you do. You need to be able to answer them quickly and efficiently because your answer could be the difference between a one-time encounter or a lifetime of friendship or business.

Or imagine you are at a sporting event, the supermarket, or even on an elevator. You should be able to clearly articulate who you are and what your mission is because, as we talked about in Kelf Key #7, you never know who you are talking to until you know.

In almost every interview or first encounter with a potential client, you will be asked, "tell me about yourself," or, "what do you do?" When someone asks you this you want to answer in a rehearsed but not robotic fashion that shows you know who you are and what your objectives are.

As I grow the Professional Basketball Combine, I have been asked the same questions hundreds of times. The questions are, "what is your background, why did you create the PBC, what is the combine all about, and what will it do for my client?" When I first started answering these questions, I thought I had my elevator pitch down, when in reality I had only the shell of my pitch down. Over time, I figured out ways to maximize the depth of my answer, while doing it in a timely fashion. I also had to learn how to answer these questions differently depending on who was asking them: agents, team personnel, media, potential sponsors, etc.

The concept of an elevator pitch tends to be focused around students getting internships and jobs and entrepreneurs trying to pitch for funding, but elevating your elevator pitch is a crucial skill to have in any industry. If you are a plumber, electrician, doctor, entrepreneur, teacher, lawyer, speaker, or actor, you need to know exactly what you do and the value you bring. You have to be able to convince someone or reassure someone that you are right for the job.

An elevator pitch can be done in many ways but I recommend breaking it down into three parts:

- Share your story (Who are you?)
- Share your skill set (What value can you add? What are your qualifications? What skills do you have?)
- Share your goal (What are you looking to accomplish?)

Your elevator pitch will change and evolve as you progress through your career and experience your journey, but no matter where you are in life, it is your responsibility to know your own story and what value you can add.

Elevate Your Network in Action: Ask a professor or colleague after work to spend five minutes with you practicing your elevator pitch. Ask your spouse to go back and forth with you. Record yourself practicing in front of the mirror. Rehearse your story and practice your elevator pitch every week, especially during interview season or promotion season, or before big meetings.

Kelf Key #14: Establish Credibility in Your Industry

"Brand yourself for the career you want, not the job you have."
– Dan Schawbel

"Position yourself as a center of influence, the one who knows the movers and shakers. People will respond to that, and you'll soon become what you project."
– Bob Burg

Do you want to be able to command meetings with high-level executives and decision makers? Do you want to have people reach out to you as the expert in your industry? Do you want to connect with thought leaders and celebrities? Do you want to be able to motivate your employees? Do you want to be a respected, go-to resource in your line of work? If you want to be an extremely effective networker, you have to establish credibility.

Every interaction and conversation you have is a chance to show that you are knowledgeable about your industry, topic, subject, company, and life. You should be able to confidently answer any and every question that someone asks about you, your career, your goals, or your business. It shouldn't come as a surprise to you when people don't want to hire you or don't listen to you because you can't answer simple questions about your journey, your career, or your job.

Chris Leggio, partner and president of Mark Christopher Auto Center, is incredible at establishing credibility. If you talk to him about his business, trends, or company objectives, he can answer any question in depth and with passion. Every time I finish talking with him, I either want to buy a car or hear more stories. He establishes credibility by being confident and knowledgeable about his industry and body of work.

The other reason he is so credible is because if he doesn't have an answer, which is rare since he is one of the best in the business, he will direct you to a person who does. Often times he will direct people to one of his closest friends and chief operating officer, Greg Heath, to answer specific questions or handle certain matters. Chris often has the answers, but he knows that Greg is the go-to guy who can go even deeper. He knows his business inside and out and leverages that knowledge to help build new business relationships and friendships with executives, athletes, businesspeople, and celebrities around the country.

It shows incredible leadership and confidence when you can admit that you don't have the answer but are willing to find someone who does. Rather than lying and making up an answer or just saying you don't know, you should always try to find the right answer. That can be done by researching, asking your colleagues, or referring the person to someone who is better equipped to answer the question. When you go the extra mile to seek out the right answer, the other person tends to trust you and appreciate you more.

With the world becoming more and more digital, social media is one of the fastest ways to establish credibility. You have the power to control all of the content you produce and share with the public when you have a social media presence.

If you want to establish credibility while you are searching for a job or prospecting new clients for your business, build a profile on any platform and start talking about your industry. Offer tips and strategies that add value to other people in your line of work and you can become a thought leader and credible go-to source on that topic.

Mike Smith (@mikesmithlive), Alexis Teichmiller (@alexisteichmiller), Alan Stein Jr. (@alansteinjr), and Shams Charania (@shamscharania) are examples of people who do an incredible job of establishing credibility within their space. Mike, Alexis, Alan, and Shams all use social media to discuss their expertise in an authentic way in order to grow their following and offer value to others. They do a great job of providing their audiences with relevant information that will help them achieve their goals in life, entertain them, and educate them. Mike does this through speaking to students across the country and sharing positive messages about finding your grind. Alexis does this by living the laptop lifestyle and inspiring women to have freedom in their lives. Alan does this by voicing his expertise on coaching and focusing on sharing tips and tricks to be a better leader. Shams does this by reporting breaking news and sharing inside information about the world of basketball.

Grant Cardone, international sales expert and NYT bestselling author, has used social media to establish himself as the go-to guy for motivation and sales. He posts constantly throughout the day offering valuable information time and time again. He has shown to the public that he is an expert and that what he does produces results. This gives him credibility and the ability to grow a huge following.

Establishing credibility is important for building your personal brand and setting yourself up to be respected in your career and business.

Elevate Your Network in Action: Know your business and yourself inside and out. To build credibility through face-to-face interaction, ask yourself every possible question a customer might have and make sure you can give a detailed and accurate answer. If not, figure out whom you can refer them to. For establishing credibility in social media, find experts in your field and follow them. Next, start creating content related to your industry. If you are trying to build credibility in finance, tweet about relevant finance topics and news, retweet professionals, and comment on thought leaders' content. Be confident in your knowledge but always be willing to learn more.

Kelf Key #15: Connect With People Using Multiple Platforms

"If you make customers unhappy in the physical world, they might each tell 6 friends. If you make customers unhappy on the Internet, they can each tell 6,000 friends."
– Jeff Bezos

"We don't have a choice whether we do social media, the question is how well we do it."
– Erik Qualman

"Social media is not just a spoke on the wheel of marketing. It's becoming the way entire bicycles are built."
– Ryan Lilly

In today's age, digital media plays a huge role in how we communicate with others. Whether you love social media or hate it, you need to understand the power of communicating through multiple platforms. Every platform is different, so the more you understand how to utilize each one, the more effective you can be in spreading your message and connecting with the right people.

Communicating on multiple platforms allows your name to be seen over and over again. It allows you to develop a relationship in more than one way, and it allows you to show your interest in many people at the same time.

When I first started building my business and practicing new strategies, I made it my mission to meet someone who was in high demand and very successful in the industry. I wanted it to be someone whom I couldn't just pick up the phone and call. I wanted to see if everything I was learning was applicable even to the great influencers in my space. I had been hearing a lot of great things about a woman named Dorie Clark, who is a professor at Duke University, author of several bestselling books, and an international public speaker.

I could have tried calling up the university and getting ahold of her that way. I could have tried emailing her from an email I found on the university's website. Instead, I set out to see which platforms she was most active on. I noticed that she was very active on Twitter, LinkedIn, and her email list. So what did I do? I followed her on Twitter and subscribed to her email list. I could have stopped there and hoped that she would follow me back and connect with me, but I didn't. I knew that if I wanted to actually get to know Dorie and have a chance to speak with her, I was going to need to go deeper. So that's what I did.

Over the next few weeks, I started reading all of the content she was posting. I began commenting on Twitter and engaging with her by asking questions or retweeting her work. Once I did that, we started engaging on Twitter and she started seeing my name more and more. I also opened and read all of the emails that she sent to her email list, which by the way were very informative. I was trying to show her I was interested in her material and expertise and, more importantly, in learning about her and what drove her.

After connecting with her a few times, I decided it was time to make my next move, so I sent her a personalized connection request on LinkedIn. I didn't ask for anything yet, just to connect with her and let her know I enjoyed her content and was excited to keep reading and learning from her. Once we connected, I followed up with a personalized message asking if there was an opportunity for us to set up a time for us to talk. Not only did I get a reply, but we ended up having a 30-minute phone call when I got to ask her questions and learn all about her journey and work. After our phone call, I asked her what her best method of communication was moving forward, and she gave me her personal email address and told me to stay in touch.

This story might seem like it was a lot of work, and it was, but it shows the power of using different platforms to send different messages and engage with people. A few follows or a few connection requests a day can make all the difference.

There's no shortage of ways to communicate. You can use a phone, email, text messaging, LinkedIn, Facebook, Twitter, Instagram, YouTube, WhatsApp, Snapchat, Bumble, and so many other platforms. Part of what will make you successful will be understanding how each platform communicates differently and capitalizing on your strengths and communication preferences.

Think about your networking plan that we discussed in Kelf Key #6 and incorporate social media into it, using a variety of mediums to build relationships and elevate your network.

Elevate Your Network in Action: Like five pages on Facebook. Follow ten industry leaders on Twitter, Instagram, and Snapchat. Send five personalized connection requests on LinkedIn. Gather ten emails from people you want to connect with.

Elevation Recap

Kelf Key #11: Do Your Research
Kelf Key #12: Face-to-Face Connecting is Best
Kelf Key #13: Elevate Your Elevator Pitch
Kelf Key #14: Establish Credibility in Your Industry
Kelf Key #15: Connect with People Using Multiple Platforms

Who is your next meeting with and what can you learn about them?

_____
_____
_____
_____

When you meet with someone, what qualities do you look for? What things do you like/dislike?

_____
_____
_____
_____

What is your elevator pitch? Seriously, write it down and start practicing.

_____
_____
_____
_____

What can you do right now to start establishing your credibility? What is one question that you are always asked about? What are four pieces of advice you can share with an audience?

_____
_____
_____
_____

What social media platforms are you currently on?

_____
_____
_____
_____

Kelf Key #16: LinkedIn is the GOAT of Business Networking

"Everyday I start by hittin' up Facebook, Twitter, Tumblr and Instagram. Sometimes I like to throw in LinkedIn for the professional shawtys."
– Tom Haverford, Parks and Rec

"You have to maintain a culture of transformation and stay true to your values."
– Jeff Weiner

LinkedIn is a must-have for anyone in business. It is the #1 platform for business networking, with over 500 million users and counting. LinkedIn is a terrific way to learn more about your interviewers, potential employees, sales prospects, or any person you want to connect with. It is also a great place to get your online resume and story in front of people who have the chance of doing business with you.

Personally, I think LinkedIn is the GOAT. If you don't know what GOAT means, I'll tell you: "greatest of all time." It is often used when describing Michael Jordan, Tom Brady, or other people who are the greatest of all time in their own ways.

I use LinkedIn almost every day to connect with new people and elevate my network. It is super important that when you use LinkedIn, you make sure that your profile is constantly updated. You want to position yourself as a credible person and give yourself the best chance of being reached out to while also telling the most authentic and accurate story of yourself.

When building your LinkedIn profile and using it to expand your network, know that LinkedIn is used as a first form of background check. That means it is vital you take the time to upload your experience and share your story using the many features of LinkedIn so that you can make a great first impression.

I see people all the time who only update part of their profile and assume it's good enough. WRONG! LinkedIn offers you so many ways to tell the online community about who you are as a person from a summary of yourself, your experience, your education, your community involvement, your extracurriculars, your recommendations and endorsements, your skills, your interests, and more.

If you set your LinkedIn up correctly, not only will you be able to connect with more people through your outreach, but you will increase the chances of people reaching out to you on their own initiative.

One of the many benefits of LinkedIn is that you can research someone before reaching out. If you want to connect with someone at the Los Angeles Lakers, for example, you can search by company name or the employee's name. Once you find them, you will be able to learn about them and their journey before sending a personalized connection request. LinkedIn also provides a tool in the column to the right of a personal profile called "People Also Viewed," which helps you find similar people. This is hugely beneficial, as it might lead you to connecting with people that you are interested in but wouldn't have found on your own.

When you send a connection request, make sure it is personalized. Some people, especially influencers or people in high demand, will not accept your request unless it is personalized. Once you are connected with them, you can further develop the relationship by sending them a message. Most people receive fewer LinkedIn messages than emails, so if your message is powerful and sincere, your chance of getting a response is increased.

LinkedIn is a fantastic tool for generating leads, finding new job opportunities, and establishing yourself as the go-to person in your industry. When building a network it is great to diversify your reach, and LinkedIn is a great way to do this through a digital platform.

Elevate Your Network in Action: If you don't have a LinkedIn, go sign up now. After you do, send me an email at jake@jakekelfer.com and request my handout "Kelf's Keys to LinkedIn" for advice on how to build a remarkable LinkedIn profile. If you already have LinkedIn, start adding one new connection every day, each with a personalized connection request.

Kelf Key #17: Set Up Informational Interviews

"Information is the currency of democracy."
– Thomas Jefferson

I've never met anyone in the world who knows everything or everyone. Every single person in the world can learn something from someone at any point in time.

Informational interviews are crucial for success in every aspect of life. At a very basic level, an informational interview is a meeting where someone asks someone else about the work they do and the person they are. Sometimes these interviews are used to learn about the job market. Other times they are used to learn more about a potential client or business partner or even how to start a business. And, sometimes, informational interviews are used to learn from experts or mentors in your area of interest. The key with every informational interview is to gather information and then process that information to further your life education.

Informational interviews are a huge part of networking and establishing a relationship. It is often your first real conversation with someone, and the best part is, they are willing to help you and answer questions about their journey, job, and company. Don't take this lightly! It's not every day that people are willing to take time out of their busy schedules in order to answer questions or meet with you.

I want you to understand something extremely important that too many people take for granted. Be polite and respectful of the interviewee's time. They are taking the time to help you, so be appreciative and thankful.

No one is above doing informational interviews. You can call them whatever you want, but no one is too good to do an informational interview or too successful to keep learning. The minute you stop caring about learning and connecting with other people is the minute you start to lose. Many professionals think that informational interviews are for people in college or looking for a job. These people couldn't be more wrong.

You should strive to set up informational interviews with people who can help you achieve your networking goals and whom you might be able to help down the road. Always remember to try and add value! They should be people who have your dream job, work at your dream company, have done what you are trying to do, or pique your interest. Once you've identified someone in one of these categories, you should reach out and schedule an informational interview.

When I was in college, I spent hours upon hours connecting with people of interest and setting up informational interviews. I knew that the more people I got to know, the more clarity I would have in my life and my career. This led to me meeting hundreds of people in different walks of life and helped me build relationships with people all across the country.

Now, I spend hours upon hours reaching out to speakers, entrepreneurs, professors, and so many other people because I want to continue learning and meeting great people. I want to gather information on how I can provide a better service, but I also want to learn more from people who have built multi-million dollar businesses and created huge charitable organizations. The more people I have the privilege of connecting with and learning from, the more knowledge I will have, which will help me continue to positively elevate others and leave a legacy in the world.

Informational interviews are so valuable because they help you understand different opportunities that are available. They help answer your questions and relieve your concerns. Sometimes, they prevent you from making a terrible mistake, like taking a job for the wrong reason or launching a product no one wants.

The key to every informational interview is to get information (surprise!) that will help you build relationships and help you find clarity in your life's mission. No one ever signed a contract or job offer or married the love of their life without first getting to know someone.

The process of scheduling an informational interview is as follows:

- Find someone you want to connect with
- Reach out to them using one of many available platforms
- Ask for an informational interview and schedule a time
- Do your research and prepare questions
- Conduct the informational interview
- Send a follow-up thank you note

I know I make this sound extremely easy, but it requires hard work and persistence. If you are sincere and authentic, you will be able to schedule more informational interviews and develop stronger connections.

What are you interested in? What is your dream job? Who is someone you can learn from? What company do you want to work at or with?

Elevate Your Network in Action: Identify the five biggest questions that you want to learn more about. Then, find five people who might be able to answer your questions. Get their contact information and then ask them politely and respectfully for an informational interview.

Kelf Key #18: Getting Drinks the Right Way

"The price of greatness is responsibility."
– Winston Churchill

"You must take personal responsibility. You cannot change the circumstances, the seasons, or the wind, but you can change yourself. That is something you have charge of."
– Jim Rohn

Getting drinks is a common and fun way to network, but it is imperative that you understand the etiquette behind this custom. Everyone has a different tolerance to alcohol. Everyone drinks a different amount. Make sure you know your limits, because the last thing you want to do is make a fool of yourself. Oh, and if you aren't old enough to legally drink, don't do it.

Before you meet anyone for drinks, think about the following questions. Are you driving? How long will you be there? Should you have wine, beer, or hard liquor? How do you act when you have multiple drinks? What is your limit?

Be your own person when it comes to ordering your drink. Be confident in your selection and show that you know what you like. Make sure to choose a drink that reflects your personality. Always be marketing yourself!

And if you don't drink or prefer not to, that is perfectly okay as well. You can still be social and go out for drinks even if you don't drink alcohol.

Different situations will call for different drinks, so be aware of your selection. If you aren't sure what to order, play it safe with a beer, as it is a safe, neutral choice.

Personally, I like to stick with beer if I am meeting with someone for the first time. In this situation it's usually best to keep it casual, and beer is a great drink to help you pace yourself. I know that if I get a beer, it can last me as long as I need it to. This is great not only if I am limiting myself because I'll be driving afterwards, but also because it can prolong the conversation. Normally when you get drinks with someone or a group of people, no one will leave until everyone finishes their drink. You can use this to your advantage if you need to buy some more time, or you can drink more quickly if you have to.

Sometimes I might get a specialty drink like a Manhattan, whiskey ginger, or margarita. The restaurant or bar might recommend a drink or I might feel spontaneous and want to get something stronger than a beer. I will typically do this if I go out with someone I already know, but no matter whom I am meeting, I am always aware of how much I drink because I always want to be in control.

A couple great drink choices that are extremely popular to order during a networking meeting are a glass of wine, an old fashioned, or a vodka soda. This isn't an exhaustive list, but just a few examples that might help you with your decision.

Getting drinks with a boss, coworker, client, friend, or business partner can be fun, but it is your job to stay in control. Sometimes companies will take you out for drinks just to see how you interact with others when you start to feel buzzed or drunk. How do you treat the bartender? The host? The restroom attendant? The valet? I'm all for having some fun when you go out, but just be aware of the situation and keep track of how much you are drinking.

There will be times where you'll be golfing or end up at a club and you drink more than you expected. It happens. Just make sure to handle your business as appropriately as possible.

As soon as you finish getting drinks or wake up the next morning, write down a few notes about the person and what you discussed. This will help you remember the little details, which goes a long way.

Elevate Your Network in Action: Next time you are out having drinks with a friend, pretend you are out with a colleague or potential employer. Order your drink of choice and see how your body, mind, and thought process changes. Remember that feeling when you are out with a potential employer or out networking.

Kelf Key #19: Track Your Relationships

"Find a list method that works for you. Doodles, bullet-points, charts, what suits you best?"
– Sir Richard Branson

As you know by now, networking isn't just about talking to and meeting new people. It isn't about doing one informational interview or making a great first impression. It is about cultivating and maintaining your relationships. A lot of people know and understand this, but not very many people know how to track their relationships or why this habit is so valuable.

You should always keep a database of who you are networking with and when you've communicated. This way you can stay up to date with your network and be on the lookout for any reason to reach out or follow up.

Investing in the people you are trying to build relationships with is going to be key to your success. Once you meet someone or get the interview you've been trying to secure for months, then begins the time to track your relationship. It's time to put in the work when you aren't in person. This is when you can separate yourself from everyone else and elevate your networking game.

There are many ways to do this, but I recommend developing a list that contains everyone you network with. Include their name, their job, their company, the reason for reaching out, a few things about them, and then the dates you've talked to them. This doesn't have to be some grandiose list that you keep updated religiously. It should just serve as a platform for you to reference as you build your network. Figure out what works for you and use it to track your relationships.

There are software systems for customer relationship management (CRM) and company databases, but for individuals, creating your own list on Excel (or another list-building platform) is a simple and great way to expand and track your relationships. It's super valuable for staying on top of potential leads in the job search or sales process.

The most successful people and best networkers keep a list of every person they meet and track their relationships. In the time that follows, they use their list to send articles, books, happy birthday wishes, congratulatory messages, and gifts that they think the other person can benefit from. By doing this, these expert connectors are able to build stronger bonds and add more value to their network.

Creating a system that works for you will help you keep track of your network without having to constantly think about it. Networking is a process, and when you establish a working system to track your relationships, it makes this process a little simpler and easier to manage.

Elevate Your Network in Action: Create a document on paper or on your computer. Take the first ten people who come to mind and input their information in your new networking document. Use different colors to track your level of relationship. For example, use yellow when you need to follow up with someone. Use green for a meeting scheduled. Create a system that works for you and get in the habit of updating this document regularly.

Kelf Key #20: Update Your Contacts Regularly

"Don't ignore the effort of someone who tries to keep in touch. It's not all the time someone cares."
– Anonymous

"Stay reachable. Stay in touch. Don't isolate."
– Michael Jordan

As we've mentioned, people love feeling appreciated, listened to, and loved. You should update your network regularly and let them know how you are doing. People love when they feel wanted and valued. I recommend that you reach out to your contacts every couple of months.

When you update someone in your network, inform them on what you are up to, but make sure you mention something about them or about your previous interactions with them. By bringing up something about previous interactions, it makes it less about ME and more about WE. Whatever reason you have for updating someone, make sure your first priority is to show them that you value your relationship with them.

Take some time before updating your contact to do your research. See if anything has changed for that person, such as a career move or location change. These little details add a human element and show you've been thinking about them. With social media at our fingertips and people generally maintaining all of their profiles regularly, you can use this to make your update more personal.

When you update a contact, feel free to ask to get coffee, food, or drinks. If you can meet with them in person, do it. By doing so, you can get their full attention and have quality time together, making your update much more powerful for the growth of the relationship. Obviously, you won't be able to do this every time, depending on location, but if you are in the same city, there's no harm in trying to get together in person. Whenever I update my contacts, I always try to meet in person because I know that way, we can maximize our time together and we can accomplish a lot more.

Other times, you may want to update your contacts through a quick text or email. The process is the same, but sometimes this is more effective than trying to set a meeting. This is great for when you want to give just a quick update or set the stage for a future meeting.

If you do an informational interview with someone, updating them every month or couple of months is a great way to stay at the front of their mind. It's an authentic way to be persistent. When you update someone with whom you did an informational interview, always try to mention something they said when you first spoke which you have utilized in your life since then. You can talk about how their advice has played a role in your journey.

If you are updating a potential employer or someone you want to do business with, try to find out what their needs are and whether they have changed since you last communicated. See if there is any new information on your end that might provide them with more value than what you discussed last time. If you have new marketing materials or there's been a change in your role, let them know. Offer to provide a solution that will be beneficial to everyone involved.

Use social media as a platform for updating your contacts on a mass scale. Reaching out individually will always be more fruitful and meaningful, but there are several benefits of using social media to update your network.

I always tell people to post on social media so that others can follow your journey and stay updated with everything you are doing. This isn't about bragging about yourself and trying to make yourself look as good as possible; it's about letting your friends, connections, colleagues, and followers know what is going on in your life. You never know when someone might be following along who has a new opportunity for you or when your posts might inspire someone. I tend to post a lot about my speaking engagements and the other endeavors I am involved in. I don't know who sees every post or how it impacts each person, but I know that the more quality content I post and the more value I add, the more updated my contacts will be and the better they will know what I am up to.

A while back, I met someone who worked in sports and while we stayed in touch here and there, I never realized he was following my journey on social media. All of a sudden, without any specific reason other than wanting to touch base, he reached out and told me how he loved what I was doing and that he wanted to introduce me to someone who might be a good business partner. Not only did posting on social media lead to us reconnecting, but it prompted him to set up an introduction which I was grateful for. Social media might not be your preferred method of updating your contacts, but it is a great way to provide your contacts with regular updates into your personal life.

The big thing to remember is that when you post on social media, you must make sure your online personality resembles your in-person personality. Be authentic in your post, but be proud of what you are doing.

Elevate Your Network in Action: Think of two people that you haven't connected with in a while and reach out to them. Let them know what you are up to and see if there is anything you can do for them.

Elevation Recap

Kelf Key #16: LinkedIn is the GOAT of Business Networking
Kelf Key #17: Set Up Informational Interviews
Kelf Key #18: Getting Drinks the Right Way
Kelf Key #19: Track Your Relationships
Kelf Key #20: Update Your Contacts Regularly

Let's connect on LinkedIn. You can search Jake Kelfer and add me directly. Just make sure to send a personalized message ☺ Who are 5 other people you want to connect with on LinkedIn?

_____

_____

_____

_____

What are 3 questions you want to ask someone in your next informational interview?

_____

_____

_____

_____

What is your drink of choice? If you are 21+ and you drink, go enjoy a few drinks and monitor your tolerance. When do you start to feel different? How does your attitude and personality respond?

_____

_____

_____

_____

Create a sample format below that you can use for tracking your relationships. (Ex. Name, Position, Company, Email, Reason for Reaching Out)

_____

_____

_____

_____

What is something relevant going on in your life right now that you can update someone on?

_____

_____

_____

_____

Kelf Key #21: Say Thank You. Following Up is a Must!

"Diligent follow up and follow through will set you apart from the crowd and communicate excellence."
– John C. Maxwell

"Follow up and follow through until the task is completed, the prize won."
– Brian Tracy

After you connect with someone, send a thank you note and follow up, regardless of the reason for connecting with them. Not only do you want to show that you are appreciative of their time, but you want to set the stage for future communication. Time is our most precious resource! Knowing that, it's your job to show gratitude for other people's spent time and energy. This goes for first encounters, experiences with clients, meetings with mentors, and even catching up with a great friend.

A follow up or a thank you note is one way to show you are invested in the relationship. Following up is not about you; it's about the other person. It's about showing them that you are grateful and that you value the relationship.

By writing a thank you note, you are telling the person that you want to continue developing the relationship and that you value their time and attention. In the job search process this is extremely important because it shows that you are being proactive. You should send a thank you note after every interview to each person who interviewed you or spent time talking with you. If we're talking about building a relationship with a client, it shows that you value their business (or *will* value their business) and intend to take care of them during the duration of your contract. It also lets the client know that you are going to be a great communicator. A little extra effort in the form of a thank you can go a long way in developing a relationship.

A colleague of mine values thank you notes more than most people I know. When she was first starting her business and trying to grow her network, she knew she needed to find ways to differentiate herself in the marketplace. She decided that she was going to be the most grateful person she could be and vocalize that to others. As she started meeting people at networking events or through referrals, she immediately followed up with handwritten notes. After several months of doing this, one of her contacts reached out and told her that she had had the thank you note on her desk for the last few months and had been waiting for the right time to hire her. She told my colleague that her note had made her day and she would be the first call when she had an opportunity. That was one of the first clients my colleague got, and they have remained close partners and friends since then.

I always, always, always send thank you follow-ups because I want the other person or party to know how much I appreciate working with them. This gives me a better chance of evolving the relationship and securing future business, introductions, or opportunities.

Oftentimes after a meeting you will have some tasks to follow up with or some additional information to send. Make sure that you include this is in your note, because you don't want to forget. People want to get into business with others who are accountable, responsible, and true to their word; well, this is a simple way to show you are that type of person.

While thank you emails should be thoughtful and personalized, here are the four things you should include in every single one:

1. Thank the person and let them know you appreciated their time.
2. Tell them one thing that you learned or enjoyed from your conversation/meeting.
3. Let them know one thing that you are going to take away and apply to your life.
4. Thank them again and let them know you will be in touch.

You don't want to just *create* relationships; you want to *develop* them and turn them into friendships and partnerships. It's great to meet new people, but unless you follow up, you won't develop a relationship. Sending a follow up after an introduction, a client experience, or any time you meet with someone gives you and the other person a chance to continue fostering and deepening the relationship.

Meeting someone one time is not relationship building. It's an interaction. Following up and continuing to have authentic communication is relationship building. Create an experience for the other person and show that you are invested in and genuinely care about them. Don't forget this difference between meeting someone and building a relationship.

Sending thank you notes or showing gratitude is a meaningful habit regardless of whether you are applying for a job, meeting someone new, or running a huge company. When Doug Conant was the CEO of Campbell Soup he wrote approximately 30,000 thank you notes to his employees and energized the company in the process. He knew that by showing gratitude to his employees and thanking them for their work and effort, he would be able to energize and engage them. This helped build trust and ultimately improved his relationship with thousands of employees.

Following up can be as simple as sending a text or an email. As you get to know someone better, you will be able to contact them in a variety of ways. The key is to make sure you keep your name in their head.

Elevate Your Network in Action: Send a thank you or follow up every time you meet someone new.

Kelf Key #22: Become Genuinely Interested in Other People

"If people like you, they will listen to you. If people trust you, they'll do business with you."
– Zig Ziglar

"You can make more friends in two months by becoming interested in other people than you can in two years by trying to get other people interested in you."
– Dale Carnegie

People know whether you are sincere or fake when it comes to building relationships. They can tell whether you are networking because you genuinely care or because you want something from them. It's so obvious—so take the time to show genuine interest in someone else!

There have been times when people whom I've never met and don't know ask me if I can do them a favor by introducing them to someone in my network. When I receive an email like that, I am immediately turned off because I can tell right away that the person is connecting with me for selfish reasons and isn't interested in adding value or getting to know me at all. Instead, when you reach out, you should actually care about speaking with and learning from the contact. You may not be able to add monetary value or even introduce them to anyone, but you can show that you are interested in what they are currently working on or their journey.

Dale Carnegie says in his world-renowned book, *How to Win Friends and Influence People,* "a person's name is to that person the sweetest and most important sound in any language" (79). When you meet someone in person or digitally, start the conversation by saying their name and finish the conversation by saying their name. This takes little effort, but trust me, they'll notice.

How good does it feel when you see someone you've met just a few times come up to you and greet you by your name? Or, how good does it feel when someone remembers a tiny little fact about you that they bring up in a conversation or follow up? I don't care who you are, it feels great!

I spent a month living in Nashville and while I was there I met some incredible people. There was one situation in particular that made me feel the power of genuine interest. Through a good friend of mine I met Joey Graham, who is the owner of FWD Clothing Company, an awesome apparel line and movement. We instantly hit it off and I gave him a copy of my book. The next weekend I visited him at his store, which by the way is an awesome VW van that he parks outside of a restaurant on one of the busiest streets in town, to see him sell shirts in action and to offer help if needed. While I was there a customer came up, and they were chatting while I stood in the background. The customer was there with his high school daughter and they were talking about math. Joey, remembering that I talk about my love for math in the introduction to my first book, *Elevate Beyond,* proceeded to pull the book out from his car and show the customer the relevant page as well as hype up my book. I couldn't believe that a person I'd known for a week had read my book, remembered a certain part, and promoted me and my book from his place of work, all during a conversation with a potential customer. It was an incredible feeling for him to show that type of interest in my book and me. I knew from that moment forward we were going to be great friends.

Since that experience, we have both been featured in interviews on each other's platforms and we have stayed in touch, becoming even better friends.

In order to build extraordinary relationships, you need to become genuinely interested in other people. You have to listen to them: their needs, their desires, their dreams.

When you become genuinely interested in people, you will notice that not only are you enjoying your relationships more, but you are learning more and building deeper bonds. No matter what your objective is, the more trust you have, the more likely you are to achieve that objective.

Allow yourself to be vulnerable when getting to know someone. Let them know you are open and willing to work with them. Show that you want to hear about their life and journey. When you become genuinely interested in others, you can build trust and respect—both essential for success.

Elevate Your Network in Action: Approach people with the mindset that you are extremely interested in what they do. Ask them questions that go beyond surface-level conversation.

Kelf Key #23: Have a WE Mentality, Not a ME Mentality

"Alone we can do so little; together we can do so much."
– Helen Keller

"No man's life is more important than yours. Yet don't sacrifice another for your gain. Always take others into consideration when doing what is right for you."
– Sheri Omens Kelfer

"Nothing reinforces a professional relationship more than enjoying success with someone."
– Harold Ramis

I'm just going to say it. Networking is not about what other people can do for you. Networking is about what we can do for each other. Whatever your objectives are, it is critical that you have a WE mentality instead of a ME mentality.

WE > me!

Too often, people fall into the trap of networking with the wrong mindset. They approach networking with only their goals in mind, such as landing a new client or getting the promotion. They see only their desired end result. It's great to visualize what you want, but it is imperative that along your journey you are not taking advantage of others but rather elevating them and trying to help them grow as well. Networking is your opportunity to bring others to the top with you.

Do you have a ME mentality or a WE mentality?
A ME mentality thinks about networking with these questions in mind: What can you do for me? How you can help me get to where I want to go?

And a WE mentality thinks about networking with these questions in mind: What can we do for each other? How can I help you?

When you are looking out for others and others are looking out for you, you will receive access to opportunities that wouldn't have otherwise been available. If you only think in terms of ME, however, you will miss out on successes and potentially life-changing experiences and relationships. Think about WE and find ways to add value and work with others.

Competition is great and while you are going to compete against hundreds, if not thousands, of other people for the same business, clients, and jobs, the most successful people in the process are going to be the ones that have a WE mentality. Clients and bosses want to see people who are abundant-thinking and growth-minded. When you network, compete not only to win, but also to create relationships because, like I mentioned before, you never know who might be able to help you down the road.

One of the best youth motivational speakers is Scott Backovich. He understands the concept of WE>me better than most. As I am constantly striving to improve as a speaker and expand my speaking network by researching and connecting with other great speakers, I found Scott and reached out to him. When I asked to set up an introductory meeting, I mentioned to him how he was one of the few speakers about whom everyone talked positively and I was really looking forward to connecting. After the first conversation we had, I realized why everyone loved him so much. He is one of the most genuine people I've ever met and he is willing to do whatever he can to help make a positive impact on others. He could have seen me as a potential competitor and ignored my call or given me just a few minutes, but instead he gave me advice and suggestions on what to do. Less than six months after our initial phone call, Scott and I spoke at the same conference and he was incredible.

When it comes to building authentic relationships, don't burn any bridges for your short-term benefit. Instead, continue to build those bridges and eventually you and your network will be able to add value to each other.

Do you think in terms of what someone can do for ME or in terms of how WE can work together to add value to each other? Is your goal to improve yourself without regard for others, or is your goal to create meaningful, mutually beneficial relationships?

Elevate Your Network in Action: Before you meet someone new or reach out to someone, think about what you can do to make this relationship a win-win. Go into every introduction with the intention to create a mutually beneficial relationship.

Kelf Key #24: Be YOU!

"Be yourself; everyone else is already taken."
– Oscar Wilde

"Don't be scared to present the real you to the world.
Authenticity is at the heart of success."
– Unknown

"Who you spend your time with matters. Make sure to
find a tribe that lifts you higher."
– Lewis Howes

You are the only you in the world. Be unapologetically you and be damn proud of it. You are an amazing individual filled with potential, and it's your duty to share your journey and personality with the world.

When you network, don't try to be someone you are not. Don't try to be who or what you think the other person wants you to be. Be YOU!

If you try to be someone else or you don't show others who you truly are, you will miss out on great opportunities to make connections and refine your own definition of success. Your personality isn't going to be a perfect fit for everyone, and that is okay. If you stay true to yourself and make an effort to build meaningful connections, the people that are meant to be in your life will be.

Gary Vaynerchuk, CEO of VaynerMedia and NYT bestselling author, is one of the most authentic people in the business world. He is extremely self-aware and always speaks his mind. Some people love him; some people hate him. Either way, people know who he is and what he is trying to achieve. Other people aren't going to stop Gary from being Gary, because he won't let someone else's opinions prevent him from living his life the way he wants to live it. He is always going to be true to himself. If you don't know who Gary is, follow him on social media @garyvee and purchase his books. Gary, if you read this, thanks for everything that you do!

Be you—and if someone doesn't like you, who cares? If someone rejects you, who cares? I know this idea might be hard for some of you, but life isn't about trying to impress other people by being someone else. It's about enjoying your life and connecting with others because of who you are.

Once you fully understand who you are, whether that is right now or further along a continuous process of self-discovery, surround yourself with people that lift you up. Find people who are like-minded and have similar ambitions as you. When you do this, you don't have to worry about trying to be something or someone you're not. You can focus on being the best you and having great people around you.

When you are true to yourself and self-aware, you are able to develop incredible relationships in life and business. Don't limit yourself before you begin.

There are hundreds of stories of people who were bullied because of who they were growing up, only to end up being CEOs, billionaires, and everything in between. Had they listened and changed who they were or how they acted just to fit in, they might not have ended up in the positions they are in now. Just because other people try to put you down, it doesn't mean that they're right. Always remember that you are good enough and that there are so many people who are in the world who appreciate you for who you are and what you bring to the table.

Who are you? What is your definition of success? What makes you happy? What do you love to do?

Elevate Your Network in Action: Fill yourself with positive thoughts about yourself every day. Be proud of who you are and believe in yourself. If you need to, post inspirational words, phrases, and thoughts on your doors, walls, and phone and computer backgrounds to continually lift yourself up.

Kelf Key #25: Enjoy Your Relationships!

"We may have all come on different ships, but we're in the same boat now."
– Martin Luther King Jr.

"If you want to go fast, go alone. If you want to go far, go with others."
– African Proverb

The final key: Enjoy your relationships. What's the point of putting in all this effort to build meaningful relationships if you can't enjoy them? Take a second to celebrate your relationships. Treasure your relationships. Be thankful for your relationships.

How you enjoy your relationships is up to you. Maybe you'll grab drinks at happy hour once a week with someone in your network. Maybe you'll go play golf with a colleague to catch up and talk about your upcoming negotiations. Maybe you'll become best friends with someone who started as a professional contact. Maybe you'll fall in love with a coworker and get married. There's no right way to enjoy your relationships other than to have fun.

You have one life to live and one opportunity to have the greatest journey you can imagine. Work is going to be a big part of that journey, so why not choose to enjoy your time with the people you've connected with?

If networking was just about advancing your career or making money, I wouldn't tell you to enjoy your relationships—but it's not. Networking is about developing connections that can turn into lifelong friendships, partnerships, and relationships.

In this book, we've talked all about how to build, develop, maintain, and elevate your network, but the final piece of the puzzle is to enjoy your relationships. When you deeply value your network, you can truly reap the benefits of having extraordinary relationships. You will have more fun, more career opportunities, and more success.

I treasure my relationships more than anything. I know that no matter what happens to me, I will always have them. The same goes for you!

Elevate Your Network in Action: Have fun! Ask your network for favors, help, and advice. Give favors, help, and advice freely. Enjoy your journey!

Elevation Recap

Kelf Key #21: Say Thank You. Following Up is a Must!

Kelf Key #22: Become Genuinely Interested in Other People

Kelf Key #23: Have a WE mentality, Not a ME Mentality

Kelf Key #24: Be YOU!

Kelf Key #25: Enjoy Your Relationships!

What are 3 things you are thankful for? Who are 3 people you are thankful for?

_____

_____

_____

_____

What are some ways you can show genuine interest to your network and to people you are going to meet?

_____

_____

_____

_____

Who was the last person you helped? How can you help lift someone up right now?

_____

_____

_____

_____

What are 3 amazing qualities you possess?

_____

_____

_____

_____

Who are 5 of your most important relationships with?
Send them a text or email and tell them how much you
appreciate them.

_____

_____

_____

_____

25 Kelf Keys to Building Extraordinary Relationships in Life and Business

To recap, here are the 25 Kelf Keys that we discussed in this book. Each one of these keys will impact you in a different way, but when you combine them and take action, you will be able to truly elevate your network.

It is my intention for you to utilize these Kelf Keys as you wish. For some of you, you may have already mastered several Kelf Keys, while for others this might be the first time you've really given these ideas much thought and consideration.

However you choose to use these Kelf Keys is up to you, but I hope that you will find that these keys unlock the door to creating some amazing, life-changing relationships!

Kelf Key #1: Be Authentic. Be Genuine. Be Sincere.
Kelf Key #2: Meet People!
Kelf Key #3: Add Value
Kelf Key #4: Be a Good Listener
Kelf Key #5: People are People. Love is Love. Compassion is Compassion.
Kelf Key #6: Have a Plan
Kelf Key #7: You Never Know Who You Are Talking to Until You Know
Kelf Key #8: Make Yourself Available
Kelf Key #9: Be Patient and Understanding
Kelf Key #10: Ask Your Friends and Family for Referrals
Kelf Key #11: Do Your Research

Kelf Key #12: Face-to-Face Connecting is Best
Kelf Key #13: Elevate Your Elevator Pitch
Kelf Key #14: Establish Credibility in Your Industry
Kelf Key #15: Connect with People Using Multiple Platforms
Kelf Key #16: LinkedIn is the GOAT of Business Networking
Kelf Key #17: Set Up Informational Interviews
Kelf Key #18: Getting Drinks the Right Way
Kelf Key #19: Track Your Relationships
Kelf Key #20: Update Your Contacts Regularly
Kelf Key #21: Say Thank You. Following Up is a Must!
Kelf Key #22: Become Genuinely Interested in Other People
Kelf Key #23: Have a WE Mentality, Not a ME Mentality
Kelf Key #24: Be YOU!
Kelf Key #25: Enjoy Your Relationships

I would love to hear what your favorite Kelf Key is and how it is helping you elevate your network! Shoot me an email or DM on social @jakekelfer and let me know. I look forward to connecting with you!

Bonus Kelf Keys

Before I let you go and start applying everything you just learned, here are six bonus Kelf Keys that will elevate your network even further.

Bonus Kelf Keys:
1. Remember names
2. Give a firm handshake with eye contact and a smile
3. Embrace rejection
4. Surround yourself with great people
5. Prepare questions
6. Take action. Don't overthink.

Are you ready to ELEVATE your network?

Now you have the keys to creating extraordinary relationships in life and business. If you ever have additional questions or just want to chat, email me at jake@jakekelfer.com.

Website: www.jakekelfer.com
Facebook: Jake Kelfer Journey
Instagram: @jakekelfer
Twitter: @jakekelfer
Snapchat: @jkelf
LinkedIn: Jake Kelfer
YouTube: Jake Kelfer

References

Frankl, Viktor. *Man's Search for Meaning.* Boston, MA: Pocket Books. 1985

Carnegie, Dale. *How to Win Friends and Influence People.* New York, NY: Pocket Books. 1998

Continue to Elevate

To help you or your school, team, or organization elevate to their full potential, check out Jake's book *Elevate Beyond*.

Elevate Beyond
A Real World Guide to Standing Out in Any Job Market, Discovering Your Passion and Becoming Your Own Person

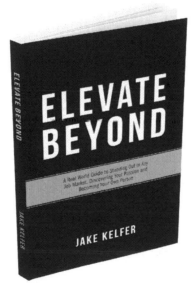

Here's what people have to say:

"From my personal perspective, Jake has done an excellent job of inspiring, teaching, motivating, and guiding people through the fundamentals of standing out and creating their own success. Kelfer's authenticity and passion to help people is evident as he delivers useful, real world stories and actionable exercises that make it easy for the reader to apply. If you really want to stand out and create a name for yourself, this is a must read."
– Keith Russ, Principal at Ernst & Young

"At a time when career and job opportunities are becoming increasingly competitive, it is essential to do all you can to show your professional and personal uniqueness. Kelfer does an outstanding job in this book by offering strategies, stories, tips, and resources about how individuals can find their passion and thrive. Drawing from professionals from multiple industries, Kelfer hits a home run!"
– Tyrone Howard, UCLA Professor

To get your copy of *Elevate Beyond* visit
www.elevatebeyondbook.com

Contact Jake and his team at ***books@jakekelfer.com***

Made in the USA
Middletown, DE
08 October 2018